PICOS DE EUROPA

ASTURIAS · LEÓN · CANTABRIA

PICOS DE EUROPA

ASTURIAS · LEÓN · CANTABRIA

EDICIONES TREA, S. L.

First Edition: June, 1993
Second Edition: March, 1996

© of photographs: José Luis Fernández – FOTORAMA.
Except pages 26, 69, 70 and 78, Manuel Blanco,
and 65/66, 71/77, 79, 80/93, Miguel Sánchez and Puri Lozano.
Cover photographs: Miguel Sánchez and Puri Lozano

© EDICIONES TREA, S. L.
Donoso Cortés, 7. 33204 GIJON
Telephone: (98) 513 34 52 – Fax: (98) 513 11 82
ASTURIAS

Distribution: DISTRIBUCIONES BUSGOSU, S. L.
Polígono industrial nº 5, nave 5, Roces
Telephones: (98) 516 30 96 – (98) 515 34 92
33211 GIJON (ASTURIAS)

Editor: Alvaro Díaz Huici
Texts: Miguel I. Arrieta Gallastegui
English version: Trafalgar Idiomas (Gijón)
Design/Layout: Editorial equip
Photomechanics: Fotomecánica Asturiana (Gijón)
Printed by: Gráficas Careaga (Salinas)
Bound: Encuadernaciones Cimadevilla (Gijón)

ISBN: 84-89427-39-9
Legal deposit: As.-729-1996

Printed in Spain

CONTENTS

PICOS DE EUROPA

The Picos de Europa are an outstanding massif in the Cordillera Cantábrica, a succession of heights which unfold from the Basque Country to Galicia and which justifies in a great deal the common designation of «Cornisa» (cornice) Cantábrica. In the corner formed by the administrative boundaries of the Principality of Asturias, the Comunity of Cantabria and the Province of León, the range seems to tear off and shape an aside redoubt with its own topographical, geological and tectonic chartacteristics; as if all the teluric forces had converged here; between the parallels 43° 6′ 26″ and 43° 18′ 58″ North latitude and the meridiens 0° 53′ 30″ and 1° 21′ 32″ West longitude from Madrid, an extension of 37′5 Kms. by 23′4 Kms., according to the authorities in the matter such as J.R. Lueje; and as if the whole range had desired to rush towards the sea to remain just 13′5 Kms. away from the cove of Barro on the Llaniscan coast, over the lands of the Asturians Councils of Amieva, Cangas de Onís, Onís, Cabrales and both Peñamelleras, of the Leoneses ones of Valdeón and Sajambre and the Cantabrian ones of Treviso, Castro, Potes, Camaleño, La vaga, Cabezón and Pesaguero.

Some say that, due precisely to its proximity to the sea, the Picos (Peaks) are called Europe since their summits were soon observed by the navigators who were returning from who knows where and this sight meant the proximity of the longed for continent, the end of the distressing conditions of life imposed by the long maritime crossings.

Others says that it was an European princess, daughter of a Phoenician king, brought and hidden in, at that time, the Province of Liébana, by an Asturian prince, who gave her name to these «loftiest white rocks». But, both one and the other are too much to say and, probably just mere sayings. We do not want to bore our readers with these and others hypothesis, and nowdays the origin of these recondit clearly eccentric massifs and, of course, neither the highest nor the most representative ones of the continental Europe, is still an enigma. Maybe due to their lack of representation, their exceptional, unique character is usually increased, for it is certain that in very few places the landscape was moulded with such violence or in such a disproporcionated manner.

Thus, it appears exceptional that the Picos de Europa could have been the empire of the carboniferous limestone, or limestone of the mountains, sedimented on the 300 million years old marine platform and, subsequently, displaced, ridden, lifted, fractured, buried by glaciers, moulded, eroded and karstified in almost every possible way, to the present. This last process of karstification (understanding the last mentioned), which makes that such pure and hard, white and greyish rocks, to behave as sugar lumps being dissolved in the rainwater, along with the effects of the glaciers, has occasioned characteristic and abundant phenomenons known as the DOLINAS, UVALAS, POLJÉS AND LAPIACES; some gentle depressions formed by the sinking of underground caves; others, craggy and sharp outcrops of the limestone among the meadows. It is also exceptionally considered the complex and great system of passages and subterranean riverbeds along which most part of the surface water is summed up, disappearing almost entirely during some periods of the year an reappering, in the form of cascades and rushing streams when the spring melts the ice. All this to the glory of geologists and speleologists who have in the Picos de Europa, from the end of the last century, the living laboratory where the teluric forces were experimented for the first time as much as the concealed secret of the waters which can be only boldy revealed.

The other rivers, the ones that do not exclusively depend on the seasonal changes to flow to the sight of whoever would enjoy to see them, result also exceptional for their capacity to break through the massif. The Sella in the western part of the Picos, as well as the Deva in the eastern, and the Duje , the Dobra and between both of these the Cares, flow encased in vertiginous gorges (the Bellos, the Hermida, the Indias de Aquende and Allende,the cuttings of the Dobra and the «Divine Throat» of the Cares respectively), like deep rifts that seem to be plotted by a trembling scalpel on the limestone epidermis of the ground. They also serve as the natural boundery of the three massifs into which «The Peña», as it is also named, of the Picos de Europa is commonly divided: The Eastern, or of Andara, between the Deva and the Duje, the one with the smallest dimensions, crags and altitudes, with its highest summit in «The Tabla», or Morra de Lechugales (2,441 m.); the Central, or the Urrieles, between the Duje and the Cares, the one with the greatest heights and roughness, its loftiest summit the highiest summit of the whole range: the Torreceredo (2,648m.), and with the Naranjo de Bulnes or Pico Uriello, as the emblem of the impossible verticality and of the massifs all and sundry; the western, or Cornión, between the Cares and the Sella, the largest of all, the one with the greatest contrasts too, with its roof of heigths in Peña Santa de Castilla (2,596m.) and with 16,925 Ha. of its surface occupied by the first National Park of the country, the Mountain of Covadonga, declared such on July 22 1918, in the times of Alfonso XIII, thanks to the Marqués de Villaviciosa, D. Pedro de Pidal y Bernaldo de Quirós, whose remains dispose of his memory in the viewing place or «Mirador» de Ordiales.

The first of the massifs, the Andara, is a large chain streching from North to South for 12Km., with a second alignment which, from the center of this longitudinal system, departs towards the East. Its string of summits, which starts from the Puerto del Alva and descends gradually towards the North, to the Dobra Valley, unfolds as an enormous circus framing the gentle slopes of the Liébana valleys and the fertile plains of the river Deva. Despite its heights being the mildest of the three massifs, it has remarkable summits with sparkling names; apart from the already named Morra de Lechugales: on both sides of this, the peak of Canal Bermeja (2,155m.) and the Silla del Caballo (2,426m.) and the massive walls that form the Andara Circus: Pico Valdominguero (2,226m.), Pica del Jou sin Tierre (2,158m.), Cueto Tejao (2,128m.), Samelas (2,227m.), the Sagrado Corazón (2,212m.), Llambrales Amarillos (2,227m.) and the Grajal (2,230m.). It could have been the relative smoothness toft its access caused the mining blossom in the area, procured from the middle of the XIXth. century to the first quarter of the XXth. century; there are remains left and not only the abandoned mines of blende, calamine, iron ore and manganese; but the place names of the area (and not precisely the already mentioned Pica del Jierro which refers to a kind of herb growing on the slopes) is,to a great extension, in debt with a certain proliferation of imposed names from the periods of the early geographic discoverers of the region in the services or, guests of the owners of the mines.

The second, Los Urrieles, emerges like a forest of crests, towers and needles, allowing to glimpse the deep and desolated «jous», the abrupt cliffs and canals, the dreadful stony passes, the reddish forks of the sunset... Little could be said of this massif, rough like few, thick and intricate, apart from indicating the majority of the terrain's connoiseurs agree -and it cannot be denied- that the massif does not easily allow to get captured by mere descriptive words, since those would just convert the bare vision of its roughness into a variegated and ardous explanation of the crazy turns of the compass to be able to orientate, more or less superficially, the winding bends that it hides. Thus, in this elevated mass spreading out for 12Km. from West to East, between the rivers Cares and Duje, and another 15Km. from North to South, between the Cueto Vierro and the Alto de la Triguera, small ranges line up one after another like the one topped by the Llambrión (2,642m.) and continue along the Towers Blanca (2,617m.) and the Hoyo Oscuro (2,417m.) and the peak San Carlos (2,390m.); or the other which uphholds the already indicated zenith of Torreceredo, named «el Rey» (the king) by Lueje, which departs from Cuetos del Trave (2,322m.) and streches towards the South-East with the peak Los Cabrones (2,533m.), the Torre Bermeja (2,606m.), the Tiro del Oso (2,511m.), the Peña Vieja (2,2613m.), the Peñas Urrieles (2,501m.) and the Tesorero (2,570m.) are the natural milestone that marks the administrative confluence of the three comunities (upon which the Picos are settled). Other ranges and small mountain chains depart as well from this main chain giving names to their summits such as Juan de la Cuadra (2,253m.), Altos del Pardón (2,137m.), and the Escamellao (2,014m.); or the one spreading out along Tiros de Santiago (2,602m.), the Campanarius (2,571m.), the Oso (2,460m.), and Carnizoso (2,460m,) towers, the Peña Castil (2,444m.) and the Cabeza del Tortorio (2,163m.); or the Pardida Tower (2,572m), the Neverón de Uriello (2,559m.), the Corona de Raso 82,148m.) and the Picos Albos (2,442m.). Here, between the Central and the western ranges of the massif main alignment, emerges from stony dreams «erect, isolated, unique», challenging its verticality, the Naranjo de Bulnes o Pico Uriello.

Finally, the third and last, the Cornión, spreading out for 21Km. from North to South, between the river Ciguena and the pico Jario, and along 25Km. from East to West, between Camarmeña and the river Sella, bulkward from the Roman times to the Middle Ages of the peculiar and particular manner of ancient Cantabrian and Asturians tribes of not being subdued. Here, in the thousand manes massif (Picos Cornión, Massif of Peñas Santas, Covadonga Mountains...) the memories of war conflicts of those times are still kept and the characteristic finery of the already renewed Sanctuary or Covadonga, a magic place transformed by the track of the times, is disposed to cult and fervour. In its heights, the «jou» (needle) appears to be the center of all surrounded by Peña Santa, Torre del Torco (2,450m.), de Las Tres Marías (2,414m.), de Enmedio (2,465m.), Santa María (2,478m.), and the Canal Parda. From this magnificient epicentre the ranges of the «two thousands» emerge in all the possible directions: Las Torres Bermejas (2,393m.) and Pardas (2,2314m.), the Tiro de LLera (2,786m.), the Aguja del Enol (2,362m.) and The Porros de la Capilla (2,170m.), the Mazada (2,080m.) and the Bolu (2,025m.) just to name some of the summits crowning the most beautiful massif.

Well distinguished, from the top of the nearby range of the Cuera or from Poo de Cabrales, in the Asturian side, from the viewing site of Llesba in the Cantabrian ,

9

or from Pandetrave and Valdeón, in the Leonese, are these three immense pieces in which this site of stone and water seems to have broken up, belonging to the living, in their animal and vegetal form, and now and always with the human touch which some of us know how to give.

Thus, the vegetal layer, considered living although relatively static, begins to spread out from 1,800m. high, like a green avalanche of seasonal colours down to the valleys, sheepfolds and inner meadows: sparse scrubs near the greatest heights, but thick, dense and of small size; little by little going down, the ground changes to carpeted meadows and the bushes take more arboreal dimensions, and the beech trees which one day, when young, ascended to such altitudes (rarely higher than 1,500m.), foretell the discountinuous strip of beech lands that up to 700m., form the most characteristic woods of the Picos de Europa: Pome, in the National Park of Covadonga, Fornos in Amieva, the beech lands in the Cantabrian Liébana and Vegabaño in the Leonese council of Sajambre are good examples of these decidous masses which turn from green to yellow, red and grey around the year. Further down, where the landscape has been already moulded by human hands making use of water meadows and smooth slopes, harvest fields, crops and small gardens spread out, spattered here and there with chestnut trees, beech trees and remains of mixed forest (ash trees, hazelnut trees, willows...) surronding villages and hamlets.

And the liveliest of the living, the prolific fauna that makes the pulse of life feel where there would only be place for being just a pebble or a dull lagoon, runs freely in its thousand ways, along rivers, over the rocks, amid the transparent air: the ibex on the needles and crests, the wolf, the deer, the wild boar, the fox, the badger, the marten and the squirrel along the low lands. The great brown bear, URSUS ARCTOS, scarce now but still errant from the Western Asturian mountain of Somiedo, Teverga and Quirós to the Cantabrian ranges of Saja, Curavacas and Peña Prieta. The colourful Urogallo, in a testimonial presence, singing just at dawn over the high lands of oaks. The hundreds of birds of all kinds and sizes, of prey, fishers and insectivorous. The amphibious from the ponds, streams, lakes and lagoons: frogs, salamanders, newts and toads. And above all, the ibex, the RUPICAPRA RUPICAPRA, that even having twice the name of «cabra» (goat), it has only its appearance, since it possesses a vivacity for the life among the rocks that not many goats do, and that usually lives on the boundaries of the high forest, although when the heat comes, it climbs up to the utmost inaccessible rocks, searching for the alpine pastures. All of them establish here, in the Picos de Europa, a noble comunity of inhabitants, magic survivors who should be grateful to this reduct of Natural History that remained unspoiled to the end of the last century, for having served as a limestone jail against the bolting inflexion of progress.

pg. 11 - Torre del Torco, western masif

pg. 14-15 - General view of the three massifs; from right to left, Western, or Cornión, Central, o Urrieles and Eastern, or Andara.

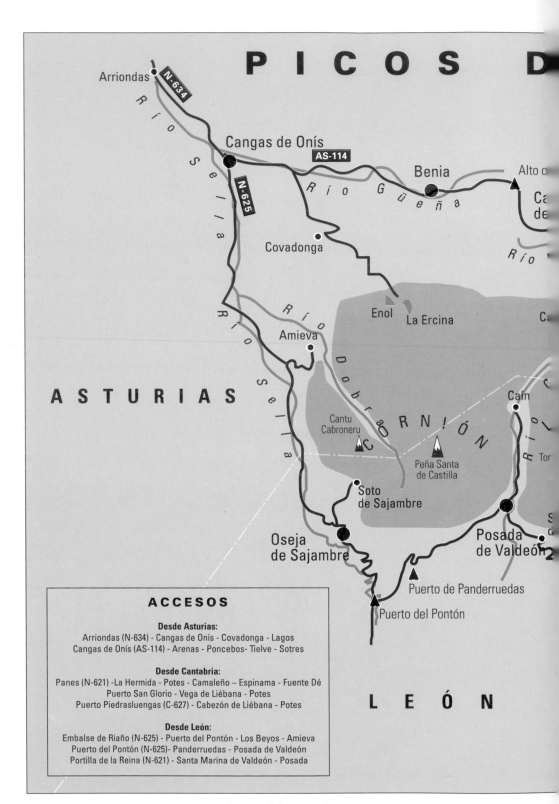

PICOS D

Arriondas · N-634

Río Sella

Cangas de Onís · AS-114

N-625

Benia

Alto

Río Güeña

Covadonga

Río

Río Dobra

Enol · La Ercina

Amieva

ASTURIAS

Río Sella

Cantu Cabroneru · C

RNIÓN

Peña Santa de Castilla

Caín

Río

Tor

Soto de Sajambre

Oseja de Sajambre

Posada de Valdeón

Puerto de Panderruedas

Puerto del Pontón

ACCESOS

Desde Asturias:
Arriondas (N-634) - Cangas de Onís - Covadonga - Lagos
Cangas de Onís (AS-114) - Arenas - Poncebos- Tielve - Sotres

Desde Cantabria:
Panes (N-621) -La Hermida - Potes - Camaleño – Espinama - Fuente Dé
Puerto San Glorio - Vega de Liébana - Potes
Puerto Piedrasluengas (C-627) - Cabezón de Liébana - Potes

Desde León:
Embalse de Riaño (N-625) - Puerto del Pontón - Los Beyos - Amieva
Puerto del Pontón (N-625)- Panderruedas - Posada de Valdeón
Portilla de la Reina (N-621) - Santa Marina de Valdeón - Posada

LEÓN

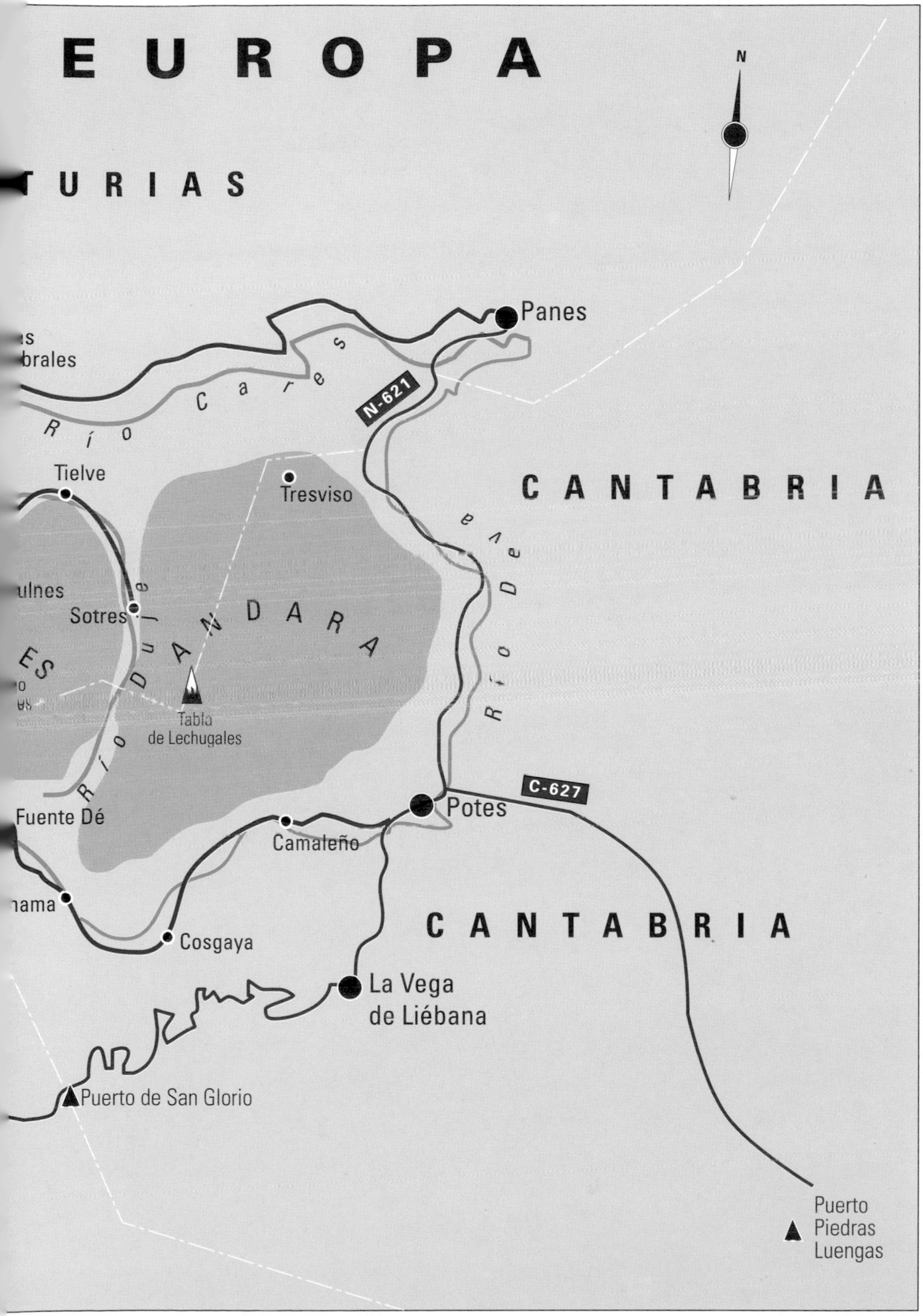

EUROPA

N

TURIAS

Panes

Río Cares

N-621

CANTABRIA

Tielve

Tresviso

Río Deva

ulnes

Sotres

A N D A R A

Río Duje

Tabla
de Lechugales

Fuente Dé

C-627

Potes

Camaleño

CANTABRIA

hama

Cosgaya

La Vega
de Liébana

Puerto de San Glorio

Puerto
Piedras
Luengas

brales

ES

ASTURIAS

Amieva and the Beyos gorge

The river Sella, along with the Dobra, its tributary, form the western boundary of the Picos de Europe. The Sella, coming from the slopes of the Pontón mountain pass, in the Leonés council of Sajambre, squeezes through the narrow and deep gorge of the Beyos, and runs for fourteen kilometres along the N- 625 road, a genuine engineering work which was finally opened at the beginning of the century. A salmon river par excellence, comes into Asturias through the council of Amieva, where the western massif of the Picos de Europa let its foothills spread out. It is in Amieva, by the Miyares bridge, where the Dobra joins the Sella, after having cleaned a tilt of 1,400 metres in just twenty kilometres. The gorge formed by the Dobra, western boundary of the National Park of the Mountain of Covadonga, located between the range of Amieva and the passes of Cangas, is staking out by water falls and pools, to some of which, such as the one called Olla of the Dobra, one can accede through a trail from the already named bridge.

Amieva is perhaps the roughest and most recondite of the Asturian councils. Amieva, with its capital in Sames, its town council in Precendi and with a parish and a place that bear the same name as the council, can swagger of being also one of the most disconcerting councils from the view point of its administrative division. But probably, the most remarkable characteristics of this council (along with the Beyos cheese, which share with the neighbouring council of Ponga) are the glacier valley of Angón, with its carpet of green pastures furrowed by the Dobra and the tremendous downfalls overhanging from Ordiales, and the woodland patches of the mounts Carombo (the legendary mount Vindio, where, to some, the Romans subdued the Astures and Cantabrian tribes) and Tornos. The well Known Arcedian's path, ancient horse passage between Asturias and León before the opening of the road that furrows the gorge of los Beyos, also passes across the valley of Angón. The layout of this path, which dated from the XVII th. century, is probably prior to the Arcedian of Villaviciosa Don Pedro Díaz de Oseja, born in Oseja de Sajambre (León), although it is commonly adjudge to him. The itinerary of this path, with a duration of five hours, departs from the village of Amieva, former capital of the council, 512 metres high, and climbs up to the Cueto de Angón (812 metres), the sheephold of Sabugo (at 1,070 metres, with an hermitage and an old logdging ordered to be built by the Arcedian himself), the port of Beza (the path's highest spot, at 1,479 metres), the plain of Toneyo (where the river of the same name is born) and Soto de Sajambre (925 metres), now in the Leones council of Sajambre.

Cangas de Onís, the gate to the Picos

Following the course of the Sella in the direction of its waters, crossing now the council of Amieva, one enters into what can be considered the gate of the Picos de Europa, at least from their Asturian side: the council of Cangas de Onís. Cangas, its capital, first court (for 56 years until it was moved to Oviedo) of the Asturian monarchy, erects itself at the confluence of the Sella with the river Gueña, which brings its waters and its riverside plains from the elevation of Robellada, at about 350 metres. With around 6,500 inhabitants, it is one of the main economic, administrative and tourist centers of the Asturian councils of the Picos. The so-called «puente Romano» (Roman bridge), which is not Roman but Medieval, over the limpid waters of the Sella, forms, with the «Cruz de la Victoria» (Victory cross) hanging from its central arch, a genuine symbol of Asturias. Almost sticked to the parish church of Cangas, one can find the arcades where a market is held every Sunday: different types of cheese, vegetables, eggs, chickens, «madreñas» (typical wooden shoes), etc., are offered to the boisterous public who overflows the arcades.

Near Cangas, in the place of Contranquil, is found the church of «la Santa Cruz», which main interest now lies on its history, more than on its making, many times rebuilt. Erected on top of a dolmen, which is still preserved in its interior and dated in the year 437. The tradition, and some historians, place in here the delivery of the Cruz de la Victoria to Pelayo (from this its name). The king Favila, Pelayo' s son, ordered to rebuilt it, serving him as a his own grave after being killed by a bear in the proximities of Llueves, a beautiful village from which a magnificent panoramic view of the confluence of the rivers Sella and Gueña can be enjoyed.

From Contranquil, and following the right side of the Sella, one can easily reach (2 kilometres from Cangas) the monastery of San Pedro de Villanueva. Originally from the period of the kingdom of Alfonso I. «The Catholic» (739-757), nevertheless, there are no remains left from that period. The whole area of the monastery was totally renewed during the XVII th. and XVIII th. centuries. The church, from the XII th. century, suffered only slight alterations, forming, at the present times, one of the most important Romanesque buildings in Asturias. The monastery outlived as such until Mendizabal' s disamortization in 1,835. Left it and forgotten for years, was declared national monument in 1907.

Covadonga lakes

Taking the AS-114 road, that follows the valley of the Gueña until is joins the valley of the Castaño and the valley of the Cares-Deva, in the surroundings of Soto, one finds the deviation (AS- 262) that goes to Covadonga, the natural entrance to the National Park of the Mountain of Covadonga. A place of religious cults (the Santina, the popular Virgen of Covadonga, patron saint of the Asturian people), with reminiscences of more ancient cults, mythical enclave of the so-called battle of Covadonga which originated the (wrongly) named «Reconqista», the Real Sitio of Covadonga is a place of obligatory pilgrimage every 8th. of Septembre, official holiday of the Principado of Asturias. But, it is also the starting point for climbing to the Covadonga lakes, the Enol (1,070 m.) and the Ercina (1,108 m.), in the heart of the Park itself. Along a very steep road (in which one of the queen stages of the Vuelta Ciclista a España is held) of about 12 km. long, one accedes to the first and smallest lake, the Enol, surrounded by plains, rough hills, peaks and «porras». In one of these plains, the Enol one, takes place every year, the 25th. of July, the Shepherd's festival, a mixture of «romería» (country festival) and «open council» of the shepherds, in which the uses of the pastures are discussed and the shepherd's Major is elected: horse races, spinning contests, climbing to the «Porra of the Enol», canoeing races on the lake, dances, cider, BORONCHUS, and roasted lamb, animate and give life to the crowd of «romeros» gathered together on the previously mentioned plain.

Two of the most well known routes of the Picos de Europa depart from the Covadonga lakes: the one which goes from the Ercina lake to the plains of the river Ario and the one which goes from the Enol lake to the viewing site or «mirador» of Ordiales. The first one, in South-East direction, heads for the JOU (a great depression of the land surrounded by peaks and crests) Llaviegu, the Abedulares and the COLLADA (pass between mountains) of the Jito, and ends on the plains and refuge of Vega de Ario (1,610 metres), now in the council of Onís. The mythic canal of Trea, falling 1,200 metres with a 70% tilt into the Cares gorge, at about 2 kilometres of Caín, departs from this magnificent plain. Also one can ascend, from this plain, to the summit of the Jultayu (1,935 metres), from where one of the best views of the Central massif can be enjoyed, as well as its vertically downfall to the tiny hamlets of Caín. The second one, in South-West direction, streches along the Vega del Huerto (passing by the Pozu del Alemán, where the German from Corao, Roberto Frasinelly, used to enjoy bathing), the Vega de la Piedra, the refuge of Vega Redonda, the pass of the Forcau and the meadows of the Torga, and reaches the viewing site of Ordiales, where the remains of D. Pedro de Pindal, marquis of Villaviciosa of Asturias, the factotum of the declaration of the first Spanish National Park and the first person (along with Gregorio Pérez, «the Cainejo») who climbed the summit of the Naranjo de Bulnes in 1,904, rest. From this «mirador», on the border of the National Park, one can observed, at the foot of a 1,000 metres high vertical wall, the prairies of the Angón valley and most part of the Asturian councils of Amieva and Ponga.

Onís the land of the Gamonedos

Going along the same road, AS. 114, one reaches Benia, capital of the Onís council. This is a council of clear contrast between the riverside area of the Gueña («of abundant and uncountable giving» same say) and the mountainous area that belongs to the North side of the Cornión, spreading out to the line of summits (the Verdilluenga -2,129 metres-, Cuvicente - 2,015 metres-, the already named Jultayu and the Cabeza Llambria -1,650 metres-) that separate Asturias from the Leones council of Valdeón. This council is, as well, the land of Gamonedos, where a cheese of the same name is produced and challenged, by many people, with the already worldwide known Cabrales cheese from the neighbouring council.

Cabrales and the Urrieles

Reaching the top of the Robellada, one starts descending to the plains of the river Castaño, which comes from the Hoyo de la Madre, in Onís, and follows to meet the Cares, when this appears in Arenas de Cabrales. Although Arenas is not the capital of the council (honour corresponding to Carreña), it is, without a doubt, the turistic center of the council. To Arenas is where the Cares comes after having pierced the Picos through all the Divine Throat; this river joins the Casaño in Arenas: departing from Arenas all the ways that take to villages such as Camarmeña, Tielve, Sotres or

Bulnes; and from Arenas is usually (although not exclusively) the Cabrales cheese, that blue cheese which is matured in the calcareous natural caves of the Picos, and which recently acquired its appellation of origin.

To the Cabrales council belong almost the whole Central massif or the Urrieles, and part of the Andara or Eastern massif. Therefore, it holds inside the highest and most well known summits of the Picos: the Torrecerredo, the loftiest summit, with 2,642 metres, and the legendary Naranjo de Bulnes, with its 2,519 metres high. The impressive Western side wall of this peak, illuminated by the reddish light of the sun-set, stands as the authentic emblem of the Picos de Europa.

The Peñamelleras

From Arenas de Cabrales, the AS-114 road runs along the now river Cares, crossing the two Peñamelleras, from East to West, between the foothills of the Picos and the Cuera range, which separates it from the coastal neighbouring council of Llanes. In its way, the Cares joins the Deva, coming from Cantabria, a little before reaching Panes, capital of Peñamellera Baja, place where it takes the new name of Deva. The road joins, precisely in Panes, the N-621, which falls from Unquera (Cantabria), cros-ses from North to South the council accompanying the Deva and penetrates again into the Cantabrian Liébana. Nevertheless, the Cares crosses before the Peñamellera Alta leaving almost no space for farm lands: Alles, the capital of the council, Rozagas, Ruenes or Besnes, are some of the villages that perch on the Southern slopes of the Cuera which forms a small valley before reaching the river. One of the best views over the summits of the Picos can been enjoyed, in clear days, from the high pastu res of this slope. The peak La Peñamellera, 800 metres high, which gives name to both councils, raises isolated on the boundary of both of them.

Converted the two riverbeds, the one from the Cares and the one from the Deva, into just one, the Deva reaches Panes, urban centre with a great tourist subs-tructure and a remarkable palace (San Román from the XVII th. - XVIII th. centuries), not very well preserved but surprising for its magnitude and the balance of its pro-portions. The river Deva is the one that marks the main routes and boundaries, not only before arriving at Panes, coming from the winding gorge of the Hermida, but also near Buelles, where the river turns into a natural boundary between the Principado and Cantabria. At the section of the N-621, between Panes and Urdón, is situated the detour that takes to Cubaña and San Esteban de Cubaña, two wonderful villages (the second was recently declared Exemplary Village of Asturias) of great cheese tradi-tion and well-looked after popular architecture.

pg. 20 - Xerra Cocón, boundery between Asturias and Cantabria.

pg. 21 - River Duje, in the background crests of the Eastern massif.

*Eastern massif and Duje valley
in the proximities of Sotres (Asturias).*

General view of the crests from Horcados Rojos to Peña Vieja.

pg. 24-25 - General view of the mitic Uriello,
in the central massif.

Camarmeña (Asturias).

Lagoons in the Lloroza´s circus, in the Eastern massif; on the background , Ataiz tower of the Central massif.

Peña Vieja, Eastern massif.

Crests from Horcados Rojos to Peña Vieja; needles Candona and Bustamante.

Central massif, from Peña Maín.

Cerredo´s massif, on the right the Uriello peeps out.

Peak los Cabrones and Torreceredo.

Two different views of the Uriello.

Overhangs into the Cares from the viewing site or «mirador» ot Cerredo, in Amuesa.

Central massif from the bridge over the Sella river at Villanueva.

Bulnes (Asturias).

*Central massif
from La Porra del Enol.*

Climbing the Uriello.

Torre de Oso in the central massif.

Sotres (Asturias).

Camarmeña (Asturias).

*pg. 42-43 - Ibex in the National Park of the
Covadonga mountains, in the Western massif.*

Counterforts of Peña Castil, from the lowlands of Sotres.

Crests in the Western massif from Amieva (Asturias).

pg. 46-47- The Cornión; Peñas Santas area.

Peñas Santas, from the lake Ercina, in Covadonga.

pg. 48-49 - View from the viewing site or «mirador» of Ordiales, Asturian mountains from the Cantu Cabroneru (Western massif) to the Peña Ten (Piloña).

Lake Enol, in Covadonga.

pg. 52-53 - Cannal Llampa Cimera, in the background, the Argaos.

LEON

Sajambre, the garden of the Peña Santa

The council of Sajambre occupies the area correspondent to the high Sella, from its birth, to the entrance of the Beyos gorge. Its capital, Oseja de Sajambre, is situated at few kilometres away from the gorge, framed by the huge Pica Ten (1,222 metres), which dominates the whole valley of Sajambre. The detour that goes to the top, to the village of Soto de Sajambre, garden of Peña Santa, at the foothill of Sierra Beza, is located between Oseja and the entrance of the gorge. The valley of Soto spreads out towards the Western massif of the Picos de Europa, resulting a superb access point to it. From Soto, a trail of 7 kilometres departs and ascends in zigzag to the sheepfold of Begabaño, one of the most beautiful prairies of the Picos, from where the already named Arcedian's path departs and where one can admire the incredible line of summits of the Western and Central massifs.

Valdeón, the placid valley

The valley of Valdeón, sheltered by the borderlines of the great Cornión and Urrieles massifs, encases itself deeply following the course of the river Cares, without other natural exit than the one of Santa Marina de Valdeón, which connects to Riaño ascending the mountain pass of Pandetrave (1,562 metres) and glimpses the Pontón mountain pass from Panderruedas. Its disposition in a closed depression and its orientation, give to the valley a milder microclimate which has allowed to grow dry lands crops, and even spot some vegetable formations generally associated to Mediterranean climates. Isolated for centuries, the council and valley of Valdeón still keep their traditional aspect, preserving, for instance, a very curios and original trap for catching wolves and other vermin known as CHORCO DE LOBOS, dated from the XVII th century. A double stockade and a cylindrical enclosure of about tree metres wide and tree metres high, form the structure of this ingenious device. Near this place, on the other riverside of the Cares, it is found the hermitage of the Virgen de la Corona, where, according to tradition Don Pelayo was recognised as King by the inhabitants of this valley. The celebration of the Virgen de la Corona coincides with the one of the Virgen de Covadonga, therefore, the similarities are numerous.

The capital of the council is Posada de Valdeón where the main services of the community are situated. The ways that communicate with Caín and the Cares throat, across Cordiñanes, and from the South with Riaño o The Liébana, diverting along the port of San Glorio at the point of Portilla de la Reina, depart from the town square.

Santa María de Valdeón, at 4 kilometres from Posada, is one of the best preserved villages of the whole council, keeping a great number of «horreos», curiously all of Leones type. Beneath it, a wide plain in which the river Arenal flows, shows

Woods of Vegabaño (Sajambre, León)

beautiful and smooth slopes with ash and hazel trees, on the right side, and a very large beech land, on the left side. Cordiñánes is the last village in receiving the sun rises due to its situation, passing this plain, at the foot of a rock oriented to the East. From Cordiñanes, a little further up of the mirador del Tombo (erected in 1,964 in memoriam of Julián Delgado de Ubeda, mountaineer and well connoisseur of the Picos de Europa) departs a path which goes into the impressive woodlands of Monte Coronas, where the hermitage and the chosco previously mentioned are located. Once the plains of Coronas are passed, one arrives at Caín, the last fortified redoubt before entering the Cares throat. Following this throat, and always on its left side, a canal carved in the stone or made of masonry, gathers the water from the Cares and takes it, crossing the whole throat, to Poncebos (now in the Asturian council of Cabrales).

Xerra Beza, from Sajambre (León).

Central massif (right) and Westermn (left) from Panderruedas (León).

pg. 60 - «The Divine Throat» of the Cares.

pg. 61 - Caldevilla, Soto and Posada de Valdeón
in the Valdeón valley (León); in the background massif of Llambrión.

Valdeón (León).

Cares gorge, from the Jultayu
at the bottom right corner, Caín (León).

pg. 64 - Western massif
from the Arcediano´s path.

Pandetrave.

Valdeón.

Riaño.

Sajambre.

THE CANTABRA LIEBANA

The Liébana is the historical and natural best known region of Cantabria; with its 570 km? of extension, on high mountains grounds, the inserting valleys seem to join at the same center: the place of the historic village of Potes. Three usually are the natural routes of access to this area of the Santillana's Asturias at the foothills of the Eastern massif of the Picos de Europa: the Deva, across the gorge of the Hermida, the Buyón, which indicates the road to Palencia through the mountain pass of Piedrasluengas, and the Quiviesa, which, with the river Viejo, leads, along the valley of Cereceda, to the Leonés council of Valdeón across the pass of San Glorio.

From the Hermida to Potes

From the Hermida gorge (20 km of winding road at the right side of the trout and salmon Deva river), one can ascend along a mighty slope that ends at the village of Treviso, capital of the «picón» (with denomination of origin Bejes-Treviso) cheese, of an excellent quality and one of the best well known in the area. This village, frequently incommunicate due to the severity of the winters, offers from its surroundings beautiful views of the village as well as of the Urdón valley.

Following the gorge, and now almost at its end, it is found the Santa María de Lebeña's church, from the X th. century, one of the best, if not the best, example of Mozarabe architecture in Cantabria. Tama is located at the very end of the gorge, and a little further, Potes, which origins go back to the VII th. century and it is, nowadays, administrative center and main tourist spot of the area; its predominant activities are still farming and stock breeding, apart from the tourism (very developed during the last years) as one can noticed at Monday's weekly markets as well as the markets oriented exclusively to the selling of cattle.

Among the group of constructions that show the historical importance of Potes, the Torre del Infantado is the most outstanding, from the XV th. century, used to belong to the marquis of Santillana but it has been now turned into the town council. Near Potes, at about 5 kilometres, it is placed the formerly bright monastery of Santo Toribio, founded in the times of Alfonso Ist., in the VIII th. century and that preserves, as certain as all the reliquaries, the LIGNUM CRUCIS, considered the biggest of the remains; on the surrounding slopes there are scattered chapels, hermitages and «miradores» (like the San Miguel's one) that used to be part of that monastic complex, organising focus of the Liébana and beacon of reference for a great part of the «illuminating» culture of the Medieval Ages, and it was precisely here where Beato de Liébana wrote his «Comentarios al Apocalipsis», of so much influence in those times.

From Potes to Fuente Dé

Further away from Potes, following the course of the river Sella and the national 621 which accompanies it, Mongrovejo, Pembres, Cosgaya (where, it is said, the surviving Muslims from the battle of Covadonga who dared to enter the Picos after their defeat were buried) and Espinama mark essential stages before arriving at the Parador of the river Deva (placed on a small valley and surrounded by the impressive summits of Peña Vieja, Peña Remoña, Pico de la Padiorna and Valdecoro) and Fuente Dé, where a cable rail allows to overcome the huge wall where the «mirador» of the Cable is situated to feel on the skin the unharmed height of the Picos and their vertiginous deep valleys. From the above named «mirador» (at 1,832 metres) one can start numerous mountain trips towards the interior of the Picos.

The Liébana, and principally the villages of Potes, Camaleño, Espinama, Cosgaya and Fuente Dé, are beginning to see an incipient tourist boom which is favoured by the splendid conditioning of the road structures.

On the road to Palencia, through the Valley and hills of Piedrasluengas, it is situated the Romanesque church of Santa María de Piasca, of pre Romanesque origin, but actually built in 1,172, although it suffered consecutive reforms.

The third way of entrance to the Liébana, the one that comes from Leones lands, looks more ragged but no less interesting: from the «mirador» of Lesba, at 1,170 metres, complete landscapes of the last redoubts of autochthonous woodlands and of brown bears, as well as the cold and white edges of the Central massif are offered to the eyes of the beholder.

Picos de Europa from San Vicente de la Barquera (Cantabria).

Peñarrubia in the foreground, Caldas; in the background, La Hermida.

Pembés, Liébana (Cantabria).

Santa María de Lebeña, Liébana (Cantabria).

Viewing site or «mirador» of Llesba

Treviso path (Cantabria). Urdón valley from Balcón de Pilatos.

Potes.

Potes Market;
on the background the Tower of the Infantado

pg. 72-73 - San Glorio Pass

Santo Toribio del Liébana

Santo Toribio del Liébana

pg. 76-77 - Piedrasluengas Pass

*Potes, capital of the Liebaniéga Cantabria,
and the Western massif.*

Fuente Dé, cable railway (Cantabria).

pg. 79 and 80 - Fuente Dé

Cabaña Verónica

Magrovejo

Piasca Church

From the viewing site or «mirador» of the Cable

Fuente Dé

pg. 92-93 - Áliva